My Mother
Is the Best Gift
I Ever Got

My Mother
Is the Best Gift
I Ever Got

Children on Mothers

David Heller

Michael O'Mara Books Limited

This edition first published in 1994 by
Michael O'Mara Books Ltd
9 Lion Yard
Tremadoc Road
London SW4 7NQ

Copyright © 1993 by David Heller
Illustrations copyright © 1993 by Melanie Hope Greenberg

This edition published by arrangement with Villard Books,
a division of Random House Inc., New York

A CIP catalogue record for this book is available from the
British Library

ISBN 1-85479-745-X

Printed and bound in Slovenia by Printing House Delo
Tiskarna by arrangement with Korotan Italiana, Ljubljana

To my mother,
with love

Introduction

If you want to find out how important and influential mothers are, just ask their children. Or even better, just listen to their children.
Youngsters talk about their mothers all the time, and they frequently do so in a spirit of praise and adoration. Of course, sometimes youngsters will offer a gentle critique of their mothers and other mums too. Because four- to ten-year-olds spend so much time with their mothers, they have a special perspective on motherhood and on how children really see their mothers.

In this collection of wisdom and humour about motherhood, children reflect on the place of their mothers in their lives and in the world as a whole. They begin with what being a mother is like, and they share their observations on how mothers typically talk and behave. The children describe their own mothers, and their love for Mum comes through loud and clear. The children have some fun with mothers too, as they share original Mother's Day cards, depict Mum's housekeeping and culinary habits, discuss what the tabloids might have to say about Mum, and offer much, much more.

Through all the amusing quips and comments, this collection is a salute to mothers and to their great contributions to the life of any child. The children help us to remember that while a mother performs all kinds of roles in and out of the family, nobody else could possibly fill her role. A mother is a very special person indeed.

David Heller

Reflections on Motherhood

"Motherhood is fun if you have the time and the children for it."
Bradley, age 10

"Mothers are like the Beatles because they got long hair and they are pretty old."
Nathan, age 10

"Motherhood ain't for me ... I'll probably be a father."
Dick, age 7

"The best thing about motherhood is nobody ever makes you give it up. You can do it as long as you want."
Jenny, age 8

"Motherhood is fattening, but I would still recommend it."
Marie, age 9

"Mothers used to be little girls but then they got grown-up all of a sudden."
Roberta, age 8

What Are Mothers For?

"They give you your allowance and then borrow it back when they run out of money at the market."
Arnold, age 10

"Mothers are there in case nobody else will marry you."
Jay, age 5

"Mothers are the ones that bring you into the world, but that only happens after God has put the finishing touches on you."
Julia, age 9

"Mothers keep the love and the chocy biccies coming."
Vern, age 7

Concerning What the World's First Mother Was Like as a Mum

"She would hire a dinosaur for the day and use it to sweep up the cave."
Dick, age 7

"The first mother was probably a lot like the mothers that you get now, except I don't think they had hairdressers in those days."
Gary, age 9

"I think her name was Mary and she was the type of mother who didn't get in the way of her son if he wanted to perform miracles or something like that."
Karen, age 8

"I bet she made her kids clean their room, and that's why we have to do it to this day."
Sam, age 8

"The mother gets the thermometer out, and if you
pass the test, you get a free holiday from school."
Sam, age 8

What Do All Mothers Have in Common?

"All mothers shop till they drop."
Tamara, age 8

"Quite a few mothers have big feet, but I'm
not going to name any in particular."
Josh, age 8

"Many mothers are too overprotective. Like my mother won't let me go to Alton Towers and ride the dodgems because she thinks I might get hurt. Can you believe that?"
Tom, age 10

"Mothers listen pretty well, but fathers will talk your ear of."
Sharon, age 9

"Many mothers take too long in the bath-room, and a kid has to wait forever."
Ryan, age 7

"They are all full of love and their children have red faces because of it."

Janet, age 10

"Mothers always kiss you when you come home from school. Even if your friends are right there."
Sam, age 8

How Does a Mother Learn How to Be a Mother?

"Mothers learn by mistakes ... So I would say they get to learn quite a bit."
Shari, age 9

"Having a baby is a big education by itself."
Karen, age 8

"Learning mother things kind of runs in the family."
Alison, age 8

"Their children teach them everything, but some of those mothers are slow learners."

Brian, age 7

Essential Qualities of All Good Mothers

"You have to be clever ... Because you never know, you might have to work out whether your child is telling the truth or fibbing."
Cheryl Ann, age 9

"Good mothers tell the best jokes about animals."
Daniel, age 7

"A good mother is somebody who doesn't shout at you for getting a bad mark. She understands, because perhaps she got a bad one sometime too."
Roberta, age 8

"A good mother knows what the answers are
to your homework."
Jenny, age 8

"Good mothers make homemade orange juice -
not the easy kind."
Maura, age 9

"They let you stay at home and not go to school
if you feel sick with no questions asked."
John, age 10

"Good mothers have smiley children."
Ronnie, age 6

Mothers and Fathers: How Are They Different?

"He doesn't usually wear high heels."
Billie, age 6

"My mother doesn't snore much."
Kimberly, age 7

"Mothers try to make your life softer; fathers try to make you tougher. But fathers are big phonies. My father is just a big couch potato."
Mitchell, age 8

"Mothers are always trying to find out how you are feeling. They care about inside stuff like that."
Cheryl Ann, age 9

"Mothers are at home more, and that's good. My mother spells better than my father, and it makes my life a lot easier."

Kevin, age 8

"Mothers teach you your manners. Fathers don't know about that."

Bryant, age 5

"Mothers and fathers are different in every way... except for how much they love you."

Carey, age 7

Typical Motherisms
(Maternal Sayings)

" 'Don't get into arguments with other
children. You don't see your father and me
arg - uh...uh...Well, a child your age
shouldn't be arguing, anyway.' "
Arnold, age 10

" 'Stop playing with that Super Mario.' "
Ryan, age 7

" 'I'll never fit into that size again.' "
Janet, age 10

" 'I know I shouldn't have this superrich
milkshake, but hand it right over to me.' "
Clark, age 9

" 'Clean your room. You have a half an hour.
Hurry up. The clock is running.' "
Gretchen, age 6

" 'Eat all your vegetables. Even the ones that taste
like wax. They're good for you.' "
Jim, age 8

What Mum Was Like Before She Was a Wife and Mother

"She shaved her legs more often."
Kimmie, age 10

"She spent most of her time in the woods looking for animals."
Sam, age 8

"I heard she was very whiny when she was a baby."
Dick, age 7

"Right before she was a mother, she and my dad were planning my mean and stupid older brother."
Gary, age 6

"She fought a lot with her brother and sisters and that's how she got to be an expert about families."
Roberta, age 8

Mum's Greatest Personal Strength

"I count on my mother for love, and she
never lets me down."
Debra, age 9

"The thing that I'm amazed at is that she
always knows the answers on Blockbusters."
Alison, age 8

"She can keep loving and kissing all day
long. Even if it's after nine o'clock."
Theresa, age 6

"Her greatest thing is roast beef and potatoes.
Um, um, good."
Hal, age 7

"She has a good personality. That's why I
picked her."
Del, age 6

"She can push down the rubbish with her
bare hands."
Jim, age 8

Mum's Biggest Weakness

"She can't play football. She should learn.
That way, I could practise my goal scoring
against her."
Robbie, age 8

"I never once saw her beat up any bullies."
John, age 9

"My mother's biggest weakness is my
father ... He's a slob!"
Sam, age 8

"She gives crummy piggyback rides."
Casey, age 6

"Mars bars. We have to hide them from her."
Jim, age 8

"My mother gives in too much to my father.
She should wear more trousers in the family."
Alison, age 8

If a Tabloid Ran a Headline About Mum

"Local mum tries to get son to stay out of the mud, but gives up when son finds five pounds in the mud."
Paul, age 9

"Liz Taylor calls my mother for advice about marriage."
Janet, age 10

"National scandal! Mum and dad are getting along too well!"
Frieda, age 10

"Mother caught saying 'Damn,' but that's the
only swear word she says."
Sean, age 8

"The newspaper in the grocery store might
say something like: 'Mrs Brown has gained
a stone!' "
Will, age 7

"Lady with three children wants to be a
Prime Minister. People may vote for her once
they taste her apple pie!"
Maura, age 9

"Mother accuses daughter of losing her
earrings but then finds them under
the toilet."
Cheryl Ann, age 9

"Mum gets big Mother's Day surprise. She's pregnant again."
Yolanda, age 8

Concerning the Relationship
Between Mothers and Food

"Food is one way they show you they love you. Another way is by helping you with your homework. But the best way they show you is when they give you a big hug."
Caroline, age 8

"Some mothers like to eat, but some are very skinny ... It all depends on their metabolisms and whether they can take what those diets dish out."
Steven, age 10

"It's kind of like they were all born knowing how to cook. It's almost like a miracle."
Julio, age 9

"They like to make you scrambled eggs in the morning, especially in the winter when you have got to go out and wait for the bus. Those mothers are good in all weathers, though."
Bernie, age 8

"To be a good mother you should practise a lot
in front of the mirror."
Ken, age 9

Vignettes About Mum's
Legendary Baking

"My mum's biscuits are good weapons. The
Ninja Turtles could use them."
Russ, age 8

"She makes some orange kind of cake, but
my opinion is that it's a waste of the oranges
nature gave us."
Arnold, age 10

"She doesn't have much time to bake, so we
get Mr Kipling's company to do it for us."
Betsy, age 8

"The butcher, the baker, the candlestick maker ... My mother doesn't do any of those."
Jasmine, age 9

"My mum should open up a bakery. Her lemon pie is the best. Except when my dad helps. Then it's just a lemon!"
Angela, age 10

"Her ice cream used to be so good. But now we just get fat-free and cholesterol-free ice cream ... I say bring back the good old days."
James, age 10

Concerning Mum and Her Housekeeping Habits

"My mother is weird. She thinks that cleaning the house is the greatest thing since sliced bread."
James, age 10

"She's nuts about cleaning. I think she needs to take up knitting so she'll calm down."
Rachel, age 8

"My mother is a great person. She is the only person I ever met who can get my father to clean anything."

Tony, age 10

"She makes up a name for every room that we have to clean. Mine is 'Operation Disaster.' "

Jan, age 8

"My opinion is that a neat house is a boring house … Of course, my mother has a different opinion."

Tom, age 10

The Most Unusual Thing About Mum

"She wants to keep a pony in her bedroom."
Sam, age 8

"Can you believe that my mother doesn't know
where a full back lines up in football? She
needs to learn more about the real world."
Michael, age 9

"One thing that is unusual is that she still believes in the tooth fairy ... She always tells me to put my tooth under the pillow for that fairy to see, so I can get some cash or a present."

Brian, age 7

"Sometimes she gets up and dances for no reason."
Randi, age 8

Classic Mother's Day Cards

Happy Mother's Day, Mum.
You're the best mum I ever had.
I hope you end up rich so you can buy me
a house for Barbie.
Love,
Karen, age 8

Dear Mum,
So what if you're fat like a dinosaur.
You're still the greatest.
Happy Mother's Day.
Your little aggravation,
Mitchell, age 8

To Mum,
If I had enough money, I would get you a present.
But I don't. So here is a cupcake.
It's only mushed a little.
Love,
Teddie, age 5

Mother,
I won't tell Dad you just lost fifty pounds on
Bingo. But that was a stupid way
to spend Mother's Day.
Ryan, age 7

Dear Mummy,
Want to make a deal? You clean up my room
for me and I'll start listening to you.
What do you say?
Greetings,
Dick, age 7

Dear Mother,
You are the best mother a girl could have.
I think you are beautiful.
And you are very kind too. I hope I turn out
to be as good a mother as you.
I want to make you a proud grandma
with no gray hairs or worries.
Love,
Jenny, age 8

A Few of Mum's Favourite Things

"Hairspray might be what she has the most of."
Ben, age 6

"She has a dinner service that she likes a lot, but we don't use it unless somebody important comes over ... like my dad's mother."
Anita, age 9

"She likes tight jeans. She thinks they make her look younger ... I've got my own ideas about it."
Alexia, age 8

"She's a big expert on art and that's why she appreciates the beautiful pictures I draw at school."
Marcy, age 7

"My mother's favourite thing is exactly seven years old and pretty as anything ... It's me! But don't tell my sister."

Ivan, age 7

What All Mothers Do When a Child Isn't Feeling Well

"Mothers get very worried, and they keep coming into your bedroom to see how you are ... Dads just say things like 'Don't worry, Phyllis. Jim will be up and Adam by tomorrow.' "
Jim, age 8

"Sometimes mothers say a prayer and they ask God to plug up the sneezing and the coughing ...
To tell you the truth, cough medicine can be a big help too."
Daniel, age 7

"If you have a high temperature, they get all sweaty and worried. That's the time to ask them for the new toy you want."
Dick, age 7

"If you have a serious problem, they'll make you hot chocolate."
Patty, age 7

Helpful Suggestions for What Mothers Should Do in Their Spare Time

"She should get a real job and earn some extra money ... Her son will love her for it because he might need some freedom."
Dick, age 7

"Some mothers like to make pâté, but I think it's disgusting."
Ryan, age 7

"There's nothing like a little bungee jumping
to clear your head."
Arnold, age 10

"They should be slaves to their children. The
children should act like kings and the mothers should bring them fruit and milkshakes."
Ken, age 9

"Mothers should use those tanning
machines. It will help them relax and get
dark without getting burnt. Besides, they
sell sweets there, so I wouldn't complain if I
had to wait."
Krista, age 7

"I think all mothers should learn how to scuba dive,
because you know how they all love those pearls."
Bradley, age 10

Do Children Tend to Be Like Their Mothers?

"Girls look like their mothers, and boys are
bossy just like their mothers."
Rachel, age 8

"I think that some children rebel and act
more like that lady Cher."
Maura, age 9

"Well, you can learn a lot from your
mother ... such as how to get your father to
take you shopping."
Stacy, age 9

"There isn't nothing wrong with being like your mother. Mine is good at marbles and snooker."

Phil, age 7

"A lot of times you do end up the same. Like my mother is very pretty and I look something like her, except for one thing that is different - I'm a whole lot of inches shorter."

Deborah, age 7

Concerning How Mothers Change Once They Reach Fifty

"Mothers are always acting young even if they are over-the-hill."
Maura, age 9

"They don't change too much. Even when they're fifty, they'll still tell you to wear a hat and a scarf. They just do it because they're supposed to."
Caroline, age 8

"I don't think they comb their hair as much, but they probably wash it just as much."
Nikki, age 6

"Their perfume might smell different because they had it saved in the cupboard for a long time."
Dick, age 7

"They still eat corn flakes, so there's no change."
Bob, age 8

Original Descriptions of a "Supermum"

"A lady who needs to be in bed by eight-thirty because she's tired out from chasing her family around."
Anita, age 9

"It's a mother with a warm smile and good brains because who else is going to teach a kid about life?"
Alison, age 8

"A supermum is usually married to a super-dad. But in case she isn't, she might have a good career she can count on."
Stacy, age 9

"A supermum is the kind of mum who can fly ... Mine can't, but she jumps well when she does aerobics tapes."
Ryan, age 7

"Some woman who has an S on her dress."
Arnold, age 10

The Children's Advice to All New Mothers

"Have redheaded children if you can. They are a bundle of joy."
Rachel, age 8

"Mothers, don't have girls! They're boring! Don't take offence though."
Dick, age 7

"It's okay to change your name to your husband's name. But if your name is·Smith and his is Yuckypoo, you better keep the Smith and make sure your children are called Smith too. Because if their last name is Yuckypoo, they'll get bullied at school."
Jenny, age 8

"New mothers should all take singing lessons, because a lot of them will be humming those lullabies, and those babies might be little, but they aren't deaf ... Know what I mean?"
Arnold, age 10

"Motherhood is not for everybody - it's only for ladies."
Harold, age 6

"Be a mother. It's a rewarding thing. Mothers and Christmas are the two best things in the world ... But my mother is the best gift I ever got."

Marie, age 9

Concerning What a Person Would Miss Out On if She Doesn't Get the Opportunity to Be a Mother

"Eating Girl Scout cakes ... But the bad side
of it is you got to buy a lot of them too."
Nancy, age 9

"Being in labour for forty-eight hours."
Paul, age 9

"You would never get the chance to spank a
naughty kid like me."
Jay, age 5

"Taking your child for his first day of school."
Ricky, age 6

"You wouldn't get the chance to share those
buns with raisins in them with your children."
Marcy, age 7

"You might not ever change those nasty,
nasty, stinky nappies ... Yeech!"
Daniel, age 7

"You'll miss out knowing what cartoons to
watch on Saturdays."
Jeri, age 6

"You won't get to see the smile on your parents' faces when they find out they are grandparents."
Cheryl Ann, age 9

"You will miss a lot of fun. You can have a good time ... Motherhood is fun! It's being the child that's the hard part!"
Jordan, age 8

"You will not have the opportunity to be loved ... You won't know that you are loved by a child who is a really big fan of yours."
Marilyn, age 8

On Why Mothers Are the Most Important People in the World

"Because they take you carol singing in December and that is an important contribution to the world."
Jenna, age 10

"Because mothers cook much better than fathers."
Alison, age 8

"Mothers are good at everything, but they shouldn't let it go to their heads."
Roger, age 8

"Mothers teach you how to talk. If it wasn't for them, you wouldn't be able to blab with your friends on the telephone."
Maura, age 9

"Mothers are more important than the President because they make laws at home that you've really got to obey."
Bonnie, age 9

"Mothers are responsible for most of the new ideas in the world, such as having people wear clothes at the beginning of time. In the more modern years, they are the ones who probably thought up things like pillows and comforters and stuffed animals.
We owe them a lot."
Lawrence, age 9

"Mothers bring you into life, and then they
teach you that life isn't as tough as
it looks sometimes."
Corinne, age 9

"They kiss you more than anybody else...At
least until you get married. But I'm not even
thinking about that yet, since I've got to get
an education first."
Ruth, age 7

"Mothers are experts on the word that begins
with L and ends with E."
Demi, age 8

"It would be hard to have children without
them."
Kimberly, age 7

ABOUT THE AUTHOR

Dr. David Heller is widely known for his popular books about how children perceive the world and experience spirituality. He is the author of a number of successful books, including *Fathers are Like Elephants Because They're the Biggest Ones Around*, *Grandparents Are Made for Hugging* and *The Best Christmas Presents are Wrapped in Heaven*.